To My handsome "Railway Man"
from his little Essex "Gippie".
17/4/2015 OBAN.
x.

STEAM ACROSS THE HIGHLANDS

BRIAN SHARPE

HALSGROVE

First published in Great Britain in 2012

Copyright © Brian Sharpe 2012

British Library Cataloguing-in-Publication Data
A CIP record for this title is available from the British Library

ISBN 978 0 85704 163 0

HALSGROVE
Halsgrove House,
Ryelands Business Park,
Bagley Road, Wellington, Somerset TA21 9PZ
Tel: 01823 653777   Fax: 01823 216796
email: sales@halsgrove.com

Part of the Halsgrove group of companies.
Information on all Halsgrove titles is available at: www.halsgrove.com

Printed in China by Everbest Printing Co Ltd

Title page: LNER K4 2-6-0 No. 61994 *The Great Marquess* approaches County March summit northbound in October 2011.

INTRODUCTION

F or the enthusiast, the best places to appreciate the sights and sounds of steam power in action, are in remote mountainous areas, where man and machine are stretched to their limits, moving heavy loads through difficult terrain. But for railway operators, these are exactly the circumstances where diesel power is most attractive.

The Scottish Highlands was one of the first areas of Britain where steam traction was completely eliminated by British Railways. Dieselisation was complete by 1963, and the only steam trains to be seen in the next couple of years were a handful of special trains operated by the four veteran preserved engines kept active by BR until 1965. For the following decade the Highlands were steamless, with the notable exception of the Strathspey Railway, which reopened the line from Aviemore to Boat of Garten.

Some Scottish branches such as to Fort Augustus and Strathpeffer had been closed soon after World War Two, but the long, remote and expensive-to-maintain railways through the Highlands were an obvious target for closure by BR, and most were expected to be axed by Dr Beeching in the early 1960s. The majority of major routes however ultimately survived, since there was no satisfactory alternative transport for the communities they served.

The Caledonian main line from Glasgow to Aberdeen via Stirling, Perth and Forfar skirted the Highlands, and the Caley also had a route from Dunblane through Callander and Crianlarich to Oban. The Highland Railway had its main line from Perth to Inverness over Drumochter and Slochd summits, continuing to Wick and Thurso, plus the Kyle of Lochalsh line which diverged at Dingwall. The North British Railway had the West Highland main line from Glasgow to Fort William and the extension on to Mallaig. Then there was the Great North of Scotland Railway, with lines radiating from Aberdeen, running as far west as Boat of Garten.

The GNS system suffered worst, with only the main line from Aberdeen to Keith surviving, part of the through route to Inverness. Some route rationalisation saw the closure of the CR route from Dunblane to Crianlarich, with Oban being served by trains over the NBR route from Glasgow as far as Crianlarich, the branch to Ballachulish also being closed. As well as the lines serving Crieff, the CR main line from Stanley Junction, north of Perth, to Kinnaber Junction via Forfar was closed, trains now running via Dundee and

LMS 'Black Five' 4-6-0 No. 5407 runs round its train at Mallaig on 27 May 1984.

3

MacCailin Mor was the name of one of Gresley's three-cylindered K4 2-6-0s, No. 3445 which was rebuilt by Thompson as a two-cylindered engine, becoming the prototype for the K1 2-6-0s. Preserved K1 No. 2005 occasionally carried the name during its periods at Fort William.

Montrose, and the original HR route to the south from Inverness, from Forres via Dava summit to Aviemore was abandoned, five miles of this route being reopened as the Strathspey Railway.

In 1972, after a total ban on steam traction which had lasted for four years, BR agreed to the running of occasional steam railtours using preserved engines. It was 1973 before Scotland benefitted, with John Cameron's A4 Pacific No. 60009 *Union of South Africa* being permitted to run between Dundee and Dunfermline, later extended to Edinburgh, Aberdeen, Perth and Stirling. More relevant to the Highlands though, the Strathspey Railway was also given the green light to run its LMS 'Black Five' 4-6-0 No. 5025 on the Kyle line. Unfortunately this coincided with the railway purchasing the Kyle turntable to relocate to Aviemore and in fact steam was not seen at Kyle until 1982, when the engine made six trips to the west coast.

Before then though, BR started to look at the Highland main line itself, and surprisingly No. 60009 spearheaded the return of steam to the main line in the Scottish Highlands with a BR Perth to Aviemore excursion in August 1980, following a test run with four coaches the previous June. A4s, or Pacifics of any description were unknown on Highland lines in steam days and this was certainly a surprising development in the story of the return to steam on BR main lines. BR Scotrail in fact planned to run steam on a fairly regular basis in the summer of 1981 and No. 5025 joined in the action on the same route on 20 July of that year, but its trips on the route were only ever on an occasional basis.

But BR in association with SLOA, the Steam Locomotive Operators Association, and the Steamtown museum at Carnforth turned its attention to the West Highland extension from Fort William to Mallaig, with an ambitious plan to promote a regular four days a week steam operation throughout the summer season, commencing in May 1984. After a press run at the end of May, using 'Black Five' No. 5407, the Road to the Isles saw four trains over the bank holiday weekend, part of a three day railtour from Euston, one departure even being hauled by a North British 0-6-0, J36 No. 673 *Maude* from the Scottish Railway Preservation Society at Falkirk.

The 'West Highlander' proved to be a great success and has gone from strength to strength, since its beginnings in the summer of 1984.

There were changes afoot in the Highlands though, with radio signalling being introduced in a rolling programme to eliminate manual signalboxes. As a test run to ensure radio signalling would work on a steam engine, before it came into use on the Mallaig line, 'Black Five' No. 4767 *George Stephenson* was moved to Inverness in 1986 and hauled a train on the far north line as far as Helmsdale, promoted as a passenger-carrying excursion.

Two steam engines were normally based at Fort William for the summer season, and the next logical step was for them to work their passage over the West Highland main line with a revenue-earning excursion to or from Fort William. It was to be the autumn of 1987 before this was to happen, with both 'Black Five' No. 5305 and LNER K1 2-6-0 No. 2005 heading the return legs of SRPS railtours originating in Edinburgh, bringing steam back to yet another of the rail routes in the Highlands. This nearly completed steam's return to all the surviving railways in the area, within the space of seven years, only the Oban line, Helmsdale to Wick and Thurso, and Inverness to Aberdeen had yet to see the return of steam.

The summer of 1992 saw one more route ticked off as another regular steam operation running into the Highlands was a series of trains from Aberdeen to Dufftown using another 'Black Five', No. 44871, based at Bo'ness. The last train of the the summer season ran through to Inverness.

The Mallaig steam service was one of several regular summertime steam operations in various parts of Britain promoted by BR itself and proved to be the most long-lasting, but BR itself was privatised in the spring of 1994 and all train operations were opened up to the highest bidder. To cut a long story short, the successful bid for the 'West Highlander' was the West Coast Railway Company, now owners of the Carnforth site. The service operated much as in BR's days, with a different set of maroon Mk1 stock and some new engines, and was renamed 'The Jacobite'. However, one thing is now certain the train will only continue to run while it makes a profit.

Privatisation brought with it the principle of 'open access', which means that a Train Operating Company' such as West Coast, has a right to run its trains anywhere on the system provided it is safe and practicable to do so.

It was John Barnes of the Glenfinnan Railway Museum, whose Highland Rail Heritage organisation was able to take advantage of this opportunity and within a few years of WCR taking over the Mallaig trains, the stock did not return empty to Carnforth straight away at the end of the season, but was used on a variety of innovative itineraries to give the opportunity to travel behind steam in the Highlands on routes which rarely saw

Three of the historic preserved engines in the old Glasgow Museum of Transport at Kelvinhall, GNSR D40 4-4-0 No. 49 Gordon Highlander, *Highland 4-6-0 No. 103 and Caledonian 4-2-2 No. 123.*

steam power. Accordingly it was Highland Rail Heritage which, having run to Kyle in 1997, and Wick and Thurso in 1998, finally completed the jigsaw by running steam to Oban in October 1999, using Carnforth's 8F 2-8-0 No. 48151.

HRH's Highland Rail Festivals were ambitious and expensive to operate but the concept developed into the annual Scottish photographers' charter. Pioneered by Bob Branch, these trains centred on Fort William, running on very relaxed timings to Mallaig, Crianlarich or even Oban, giving dedicated photographers who had pre-booked their seats, maximum opportunities to photograph steam in the Highlands, a pre-requisite always being an authentic BR black locomotive, preferably of LNER origin, and a set of maroon Mk1 coaches. The scope of these trains has reduced somewhat in recent years, and organisation has passed to John Hunt of the North Eastern Locomotive Preservation Group and James Shuttleworth from West Coast Railways, but when the weather has been favourable, some memorable images have been recorded.

It was the late George Hinchcliffe of Steamtown at Carnforth who came up with the idea of a multi-day, multi-engined steam railtour from one end of Great Britain to the other but it was Nigel Dobbing of the Railway Touring Company who got the idea off the ground, in association with West Coast Railways. It was this concept which really seemed to seal the future of steam in the Highlands away from the Mallaig line. In April 2007, the RTC 'Great Britain' left Paddington for Penzance, and from Penzance it was to be steam-hauled right through to Thurso. Although envisaged as a one-off, it was financially and operationally successful, and has run in different forms every spring subsequently, giving a regular dose of steam over the Highland main line and to Kyle of Lochalsh on at least one occasion annually, plus steam on the far north line on an occasional basis.

Kyle of Lochalsh had not seen steam between 1982 and 1997, and the Far North line had seen steam only in 1986 and 1998. Now it looked as if we may not have to wait quite as long between trains on such routes.

In 2011, Steam Dreams also promoted a similar grand tour, starting in Kent, which ran to Fort William and Mallaig, while 2012 saw the RTC 'Great Britain V' run in two portions from Thornton Junction, giving the opportunity to travel with steam on the Highland and Kyle lines, and the West Highland line plus the extension to Mallaig all on one trip. Not to be outdone, the 2012 run of Steam Dreams' 'Cathedrals Explorer' brought the newly-built LNER A1 Pacific No. 60163 *Tornado* to the Highland main line, particularly appropriate since it was an LNER Pacific which had brought the sights and sounds of main line steam back to the Highlands 32 years before.

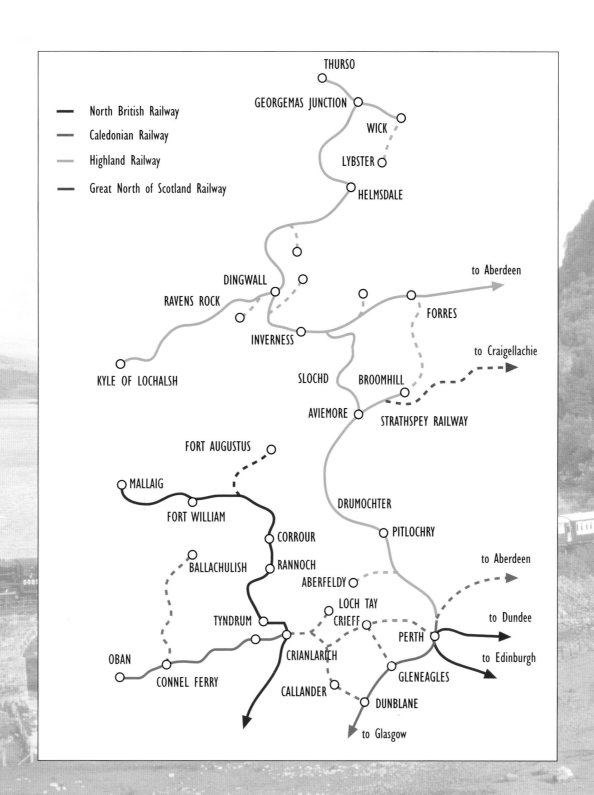

THURSO

GEORGEMAS JUNCTION

WICK

LYBSTER

HELMSDALE

to Aberdeen

DINGWALL

RAVENS ROCK

FORRES

INVERNESS

to Craigellachie

KYLE OF LOCHALSH

SLOCHD

BROOMHILL

AVIEMORE

STRATHSPEY RAILWAY

FORT AUGUSTUS

MALLAIG

DRUMOCHTER

FORT WILLIAM

CORROUR

PITLOCHRY

BALLACHULISH

RANNOCH

to Aberdeen

ABERFELDY

LOCH TAY

TYNDRUM

CRIEFF

to Dundee

PERTH

OBAN

CRIANLARICH

to Edinburgh

CONNEL FERRY

CALLANDER

GLENEAGLES

DUNBLANE

to Glasgow

North British Railway

Caledonian Railway

Highland Railway

Great North of Scotland Railway

RETURN TO STEAM: HIGHLAND MAIN LINE

Just before the persistent rain set in, LNER A4 Pacific No. 60009 *Union of South Africa* heads the nine coach BR-sponsored 'Osprey Express' from Edinburgh to Aviemore on 31 August 1980, near Stanley Junction where the Forfar line once diverged from the Highland line to Inverness north of Perth.

LMS 'Black Five' 4-6-0 No. 5025 heads Scotrail's 'Speyside Express' past Dalnacardoch on the climb to Drumochter summit on 20 July 1981. JOHN TITLOW

The summit board at Drumochter.

RETURN TO STEAM: KYLE OF LOCHALSH

Strathspey Railway-based LMS 'Black Five' 4-6-0 No. 5025 departs from Inverness for Kyle of Lochalsh on 4 October 1982, with a private charter for the Toyota motor company using rolling stock from Steamtown at Carnforth.

No. 5025 crosses the River Ness on 4 October 1982. These four coach trains ran on four consecutive days conveying guests to the Isle of Skye. The locomotive returned light engine with the stock being attached to the afternoon service train.

LMS 'Black Five' 4-6-0 No. 5025 crosses the River Bran at the end of Loch a' Chuilinn as it approaches Achanalt on 5 October 1982.

No. 5025 is seen between Achanalt and Achnasheen on 5 October 1982.

LMS 'Black Five' 4-6-0 No. 5025 departs from Achnasheen on 5 October 1982.

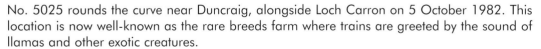

No. 5025 rounds the curve near Duncraig, alongside Loch Carron on 5 October 1982. This location is now well-known as the rare breeds farm where trains are greeted by the sound of llamas and other exotic creatures.

RETURN TO STEAM: WEST HIGHLAND MALLAIG EXTENSION

LMS 'Black Five' 4-6-0 No. 5407 departs from Fort William for Mallaig on 27 May 1984, in conjunction with a railtour from Euston, and the precursor to a regular series of trips from Fort William to Mallaig operated by BR Scotrail.

No. 5407 passes Fort William shed as it heads for the Lochy bridge on its way to Mallaig on 27 May 1984.

LMS 'Black Five' 4-6-0 No. 5407 crosses Glenfinnan viaduct on 27 May 1984.

LMS 'Black Five' 4-6-0 No. 5407 rounds the western end of Loch Eilt on the approach to Lochailort on 28 May 1984.

Climbing away from Lochailort, No. 5407 passes Polnish on 27 May 1984.

LMS 'Black Five' 4-6-0 No. 5407 runs round its train at Mallaig on 27 May 1984, before the introduction of radio signalling on the line.

No. 5407 departs tender-first from Mallaig on 27 May 1984, before the road was built on the seaward side of the railway.

The Scottish Railway Preservation Society's North British Railway J36 0-6-0 No. 673 *Maude* climbs away from the viaduct towards Glenfinnan on 28 May 1984.

No. 673 *Maude* heads west from Glenfinnan on 28 May 1984.

Now running very late as a result of causing serious lineside fires around Beasdale, the J36 crosses the causeway at the western end of Loch Eilt with the return train to Fort William on 28 May 1984.

Maude reaches the west coast and crosses Loch nan-Uamh viaduct on 28 May 1984.

By 1986, BR had repainted the regular set of Mk1 coaches into LNER Tourist Stock green & cream livery. LMS 'Black Five' 4-6-0 No. 44932 stands at Fort William station on 1 September 1986. The area to the right is unrecognisable today.

LMS 'Black Five' 4-6-0 No. 44932 crosses Banavie swing bridge with an SRPS excursion from Fort William to Mallaig, which had originated from Ayr on 30 August 1986.

At the start of the fourth season of BR's 'West Highlander' excursions to Mallaig, LMS 'Black Five' 4-6-0 No. 5305 accelerates away from Mallaig Junction, Fort William, on 24 May 1987.

LMS 'Black Five' 4-6-0 No. 5305 approaches Arienskill at the west end of Loch Eilt on 24 May 1987. The 2895ft Rois-Bheinn towers in the background.

Matched with the LNER-liveried stock, LNER K1 2-6-0 No. 2005 runs alongside Loch Eilt on 1 September 1987.

Fridays saw an early morning steam-hauled run of the 'Royal Scotsman' luxury touring train, of mainly vintage stock. With Ben Nevis in the background, LNER K1 2-6-0 No. 2005 passes Camus-na-ha alongside Loch Eil on 2 September 1987.

No. 2005 climbs away from Glenfinnan viaduct with the 'Royal Scotsman' on 2 September 1987.

With the islands of Rhum, Eigg and Muck clearly visible, LNER K1 2-6-0 No. 2005 drops down from the summit at Arisaig past Kinloid on 3 September 1987.

Carrying *MacCailin Mor* nameplates, No. 2005 approaches the summit just beyond Arisaig on 5 September 1987 with a SRPS excursion which had originated from Edinburgh.

An additional working on the same day in connection with a four day BR excursion from St Pancras, saw LMS 'Black Five' 4-6-0 No. 5305 starting the climb from sea level at Loch Eil up to Glenfinnan.

LNER K1 2-6-0 No. 2005 departs from Fort William on 6 September 1987 with the 'West Highlander'.

No. 4767 is seen on the east coast near Invergordon on 31 August 1986. This train was run by BR principally to test the operation of radio signalling with steam traction, but was promoted as a public excursion.

The Far North line saw a steam working from Inverness as far as Helmsdale on 31 August 1986. LMS 'Black Five' 4-6-0 No. 4767 *George Stephenson* crosses Invershin viaduct on the outward run.

RETURN TO STEAM: WEST HIGHLAND MAIN LINE

The first preservation-era steam hauled passenger train on the West Highland main line south from Fort William, headed by LMS 'Black Five' 4-6-0 No. 5305, passes the chapel on the hilltop beyond Monessie on 17 October 1987.

No. 5305 arrives at Tulloch on 17 October 1987. The train was the SRPS 'Jacobite' returning to Edinburgh.

No. 5305 heads south away from Crianlarich on 17 October 1987.

The second southbound train over the West Highland main line saw bright wintry conditions. LNER K1 2-6-0 No. 2005 is high on Rannoch Moor near Gortan sidings with the SRPS 'Lochaber' returning to Edinburgh on 14 November 1987.

LNER K1 2-6-0 No. 2005 heads towards Bridge of Orchy at Gortan.

LMS 'Black Five' 4-6-0 No. 5305 crosses the first viaduct on the Horseshoe Curve on 23 September 1989, with a four-coach private charter operated by Inter-City.

After a season on the Mallaig line, LMS 'Black Five' 4-6-0 No. 44871 climbs past Fersit on the approach to Tulloch on 16 October 1993 with an SRPS tour returning from Fort William to Edinburgh.

LMS 'Black Five' 4-6-0 No. 5407 departs from Bridge of Orchy on 24 October 1992 with an SRPS tour returning from Fort William to Edinburgh.

Rannoch station on the NBR West Highland main line.

Against a backdrop of snow-capped 2948ft Ben Odhar, LMS 'Black Five' 4-6-0 No. 5407 climbs out of the Horseshoe Curve on 24 October 1992.

In dramatic autumn weather, LNER K1 2-6-0 No. 2005 is on 'Royal Scotsman' duties at Glenfinnan 28 October 1987.

No. 2005 makes the climb towards Arisaig past Kinloid, returning tender-first from Mallaig on 28 October 1987.

LMS 'Black Five' 4-6-0 No. 44871 departs from Fort William on 26 April 1989, with the 'Royal Scotsman' luxury touring train.

No. 44871 emerges from the short tunnel near Lochailort.

Crossing the swing bridge over the Caledonian Canal at Banavie early in the morning of 2 September 1989, is LMS 'Black Five' 4-6-0 No. 5305 with the LCGB 'West Highlander No. 7' tour which had originated in Leeds.

The weather is perfect as No. 5305 climbs away from Arisaig on 2 September 1989.

Immaculate as always, No. 5305 climbs away from Glenfinnan viaduct.

'Black Five' No. 5305 accelerates away from Glenfinnan on 10 September 1989.

No. 5305 drops down from Arisaig summit past Kinloid on 10 September 1989.

CREW TRAINING

In order to train additional footplate crews on steam, BR ran a series of crew training trips for four weeks using withdrawn Mk1 stock. The dates chosen in November / December 1989 proved to be some of the coldest on record. LMS 'Black Five' 4-6-0 No. 5305 sets off from Fort William on 5 December 1989.

Leaving a trail of exhaust in the freezing air, No. 5305 crosses the Lochy bridge on 1 December 1989.

With the line in the shadow of the mountains from just beyond Glenfinnan right through to Lochailort, the one sunny location at the S-bend west of Glenfinnan, sees No. 5305 blowing a smoke ring. 5 December 1989.

Much of the route suffered from freezing fog on 5 December, but having been delayed by a BBC filming job for *Songs of Praise* at Locheilside, it just clears as LMS 'Black Five' 4-6-0 No. 5305 climbs away from Glenfinnan viaduct.

Seen from above the first tunnel at Beasdale, LMS 'Black Five' 4-6-0 No. 5305 crosses the distant Loch-nan-Uamh viaduct on 1 December 1989.

A few minutes later, No. 5305 rounds the curve on the approach to the tunnel at Beasdale. The coaching stock for these trains had been withdrawn from normal service and had suffered from some vandalism.

Grampian Railtours ran a regular 'Northern Belle' steam operation out of Aberdeen in the summer of 1992. On the last day, the service was extended to Inverness and LMS 'Black Five' 4-6-0 No. 44871 is seen passing Nairn on 6 September.

The following day, the Bo'ness-based 'Black Five' took the SRPS coaching stock back to Bo'ness and is seen departing from Perth.

No. 44871 passes Gleneagles with the Aberdeen – Bo'ness empty stock train on 7 September 1992.

No. 44871 departs from Stirling on 7 September 1992.

The West Highland line celebrated its centenary in August 1994 and LNER K4 2-6-0 No. 3442 *The Great Marquess* and LNER K1 2-6-0 No. 2005 joined forces for a northbound steam working to Fort William. The two engines are seen on shed on 9 August. Sir Nigel Gresley's six K4s were specifically designed for the West Highland line, but in practice were largely displaced by other classes after relatively few years' service on the line.

No. 3442 and No. 2005 also doubleheaded the 'West Highlander' to Mallaig for three days, facing out of Mallaig. The pair dig in to the climb away from the terminus on 10 August 1994, the new road now having been completed on the seaward side of the railway.

LNER K4 2-6-0 No. 3442 *The Great Marquess* and LNER K1 2-6-0 No. 2005 climb away from Loch nan-Uamh above the waters of Loch Dubh on 10 August 1994.

The pair climb away from Glenfinnan viaduct on 10 August 1994. The coaching stock was painted into authentic maroon livery for the last couple of years of BR operation.

Changes are evident at Kinloid on 8 August 1994 as LNER K1 2-6-0 No. 2005 faces out of Mallaig and the 'Royal Scotsman' is now formed of more modern stock, including Metropolitan-Cammell Pullman cars.

Still facing towards Fort William, LNER K1 2-6-0 No. 2005 emerges from the tunnel and crosses Loch-nan-Uamh viaduct on 20 September 1994.

On 16 October 1994, an additional run of the 'West Highlander' was organised by the K1's owners, the North Eastern Locomotive Preservation Group, with additional stops, for the benefit of photographers. Blessed with perfect autumn sunshine, No. 2005 passes the rock face near Lochailort, a location rarely seen with a favourable angle of sunlight.

No. 2005 approaches the summit beyond Morar before dropping down into Mallaig on 16 October 1994.

WEST COAST RAILWAYS

After Privatisation of the British Railways system in 1994, the West Coast Railway Company successfully tendered to operate the regular steam train to Mallaig, using its own maroon-liveried Mk1 coaches. A frequent performer on the line was BR Standard 4MT 4-6-0 No. 75014, a class of engine never seen in steam days. The Standard departs from Fort William and passes green-liveried No. D6608 on 20 September 1996.

No. 75014 runs alongside Loch Eil at Fassfern with West Coast's 'Jacobite' service on 18 September 1996.

BR Standard 4MT 4-6-0 No. 75014 makes the climb from the viaduct to Glenfinnan station on 19 September 1996.

The 4MT rounds the curve at the west end of Loch Eilt on 18 September 1996.

An unusual sight at Glenfinnan is West Coast Railways Carnforth-based LMS 8F 2-8-0 No. 48151, pressed into service in the absence of any more suitable locomotives in September 1997.

Another change was the repainting of the LNER K1 2-6-0 into BR black livery as No. 62005 and the fitting of *Lord of the Isles* nameplates. The K1 approaches Beasdale tunnel on 25 August 2002.

In a remarkable sight, LNER B1 4-6-0 No. 61264 departs from Fort William on 25 June 2003, passing Deltic D9009 *Alycidon* at the head of a railtour of Scotland also operated by West Coast Railways with maroon stock.

No. 62005 climbs away from Glenfinnan towards Mallaig.

LNER K1 2-6-0 No. 62005 fresh from overhaul at Carnforth, crosses Glenfinnan viaduct with 'The Jacobite' on 21 May 2012.

'HOGWARTS EXPRESS' AND THE MOUNTAIN OF FIRE!

GWR 4-6-0 No. 5972 *Olton Hall* as *Hogwarts Castle* stands in Glenfinnan station during filming of *Harry Potter and the Prisoner of Azkaban* on 22 February 2003. ROBIN JONES

No. 5972 *Olton Hall* as *Hogwarts Castle* performed runpasts at Glenfinnan for filming by Warner Brothers, but while the location can normally be relied on for the dull, misty conditions required, on this occasion it was sunny and tinder-dry, resulting in an unscripted mountain of fire.
ROBIN JONES

The 1994 photographers' charter paved the way for more ambitious programmes, organised by Bob Branch in conjunction with West Coast Railways. LNER K1 2-6-0 No. 62005 climbs away from Glenfinnan early in the morning of 7 October 2003.

'No. 62012' climbs towards Polnish above the waters of Loch Dubh in October 2004.

October 2004 saw a memorable photographers' charter with excellent weather. LNER K1 2-6-0 No. 62005 is seen at Mallaig station in the guise of No. 62012.

LNER B1 4-6-0 No. 1264 had run on the Mallaig line in LNER green livery but in 2004 is seen in BR black as No. 61264 at Glenfinnan on 8 October. B1s were regular engines on West Highland services in the 1950s but not frequently used on the Mallaig extension.

The 3524ft Ben Dorain towers above as No. 61264 approaches County March summit on 29 September 2001 en route to Crianlarich.

LMS 'Black Five' 4-6-0 No. 45407 running as Eastfield shed's No. 44996 rounds the curve above the top of Loch Trieg and approaches Corrour in October 2004.

LMS 'Black Five' 4-6-0 No. 45407 as No. 44996 approaches the summit at Corrour, 1350 feet above sea level.

The Caledonian Railway's Dalmally station on the surviving part of the Callander & Oban line west of Crianlarich.

Ballachulish station, the terminus of the closed CR branch from Connel Ferry on the Oban line is now a doctors' surgery.

The impressive bridge at Connel Ferry once carried the Ballachulish branch as well as the road.

LMS 'Black Five' 4-6-0 No. 45407 departs from Oban with a railtour from Glasgow on 5 September 2010. BEN COLLIER

Glenoglehead viaduct on the Callander & Oban line. With closure already imminent a serious landslip occurred near to this point, leading to the railway closing a few weeks prematurely.

LNER K4 2-6-0 No. 61994 *The Great Marquess* runs light engine towards Perth past Blackford on 10 April 2007.

Shortly afterwards, LNER A4 Pacific No. 60009 *Union of South Africa* passes with the Railway Touring Company's 'Great Britain' railtour which had been steam-hauled all the way from Penzance.

The Great Marquess and *Union of South Africa* joined forces at Perth to head north over the Highland main line, seen north of Dunkeld.

The doubleheader is seen at Dalnaspidal on the climb to Drumochter.

No. 61994 and No. 60009 paused for water at Kingussie, before setting off for the climb to Slochd summit.

The summit board at Slochd.

The 'Great Britain' ran with steam all the way to Thurso and sets off from Inverness behind LMS 8F 2-8-0 No. 48151 on 12 April 2007.

No. 48151 heads north away from Dunrobin with the Duke of Sutherland's castle visible to the left.

Sadly the impressive viaduct over the Kyle of Sutherland was in the process of being painted as the 8F crossed it between Culrain and Invershin.

No. 48151 tackles the long climb from Helmsdale to Forsinard and passes Kildonan.

Having arrived at Thurso six hours late, the journey south next day was tender-first with assistance from a diesel on the rear. No. 48151 is on the climb from Rogart near Acheilidh on 13 April.

LMS 8F 2-8-0 No. 48151 runs alongside the Dornoch Firth approaching Tain on 13 April 2007.

Inverness on the evening of 13 April 2007, saw the remarkable sight of three engines in steam, LNER A4 Pacific No. 60009 *Union of South Africa*, LNER K4 2-6-0 No. 61994 *The Great Marquess* and LMS 8F 2-8-0 No. 48151.

No. 60009 *Union of South Africa* and No. 61994 *The Great Marquess* depart from Inverness at 5.50am on 14 April 2007; they will work the train as far as Perth, from where a diesel will take it on to King's Cross.

With little sign of the Highlands, *Union of South Africa* and *The Great Marquess* pass Insh, south of Aviemore.

The pair are on the long southbound climb from Aviemore to Drumochter, passing Crubenmore on 14 April 2007.

No. 60009 *Union of South Africa* and No. 61994 *The Great Marquess* emerge from Kingswood tunnel approaching Murthly.

Union of South Africa and *The Great Marquess* approach the summit at Drumochter, 1484ft above sea level.

Although the 'Great Britain' railtour was not repeated in 2008, the Railway Touring Company's 'North Briton' ran steam-hauled from King's Cross to Kyle of Lochalsh. In driving sleet, LMS 'Black Five' 4-6-0 No. 45407 and A4 Pacific No. 60009 *Union of South Africa* climb towards Drumochter northbound on 13 Apri.

Against a backdrop of the snow-capped 2821ft Sgurr a'Mhuilinn, No. 45407 crosses the River Bran at the end of Loch a'Chuilinn on the approach to Achanalt.

No. 45407 was matched with an unfortunate set of stock, but makes a fine sight at the eastern end of Loch Carron, near Attadale.

LMS 'Black Five' 4-6-0 No. 45407 arrives at Kyle of Lochalsh with the 'North Briton' on 14 April 2008.

LMS 'Black Five' 4-6-0 No. 45407 faces the Isle of Skye as it draws into the terminus at Kyle of Lochalsh.

The 'Black Five' having been removed, No. 60009 departs from Perth for Glasgow.

LMS 'Black Five' 4-6-0 No. 45407 and A4 Pacific No. 60009 *Union of South Africa* climb towards Slochd summit with the southbound 'North Briton' on 15 April 2008.

STRATHSPEY RAILWAY

The Strathspey Railway is the only standard gauge preserved steam railway in the Highlands. Caledonian Railway 812 class 3F McIntosh Goods 0-6-0 No. 828 arrives at Boat of Garten from Broomhill.

No. 828 departs from the Highland Railway station at Boat of Garten on 27 October 2010. The Great North of Scotland Railway's original Speyside line ran parallel with the HR to Boat of Garten from near Broomhill.

LMS Ivatt 2MT mogul No. 46512 departs from Boat of Garten for Broomhill on 20 April 2011

Caledonian Railway 3F McIntosh Goods 0-6-0 No. 828 arrives at Broomhill on 28 October 2010.

Blacksboat station on the GNSR Speyside line from Boat of Garten to Craigellachie. Substantial parts of former GNS trackbeds are now in use as long-distance footpaths.

The GNS station at Knockando was taken over by the nearby Tamdhu distillery and renamed for use as a visitor centre, but is now disused. This line ran through Craigellachie and joined the Keith & Dufftown line at Dufftown, itself now a heritage line but operated by diesel power.

Barclay 0-4-0ST No. 2073 of 1939 which worked until the 1960s at Dailuaine distillery on the GNS Speyside line is preserved at the John Dewar distillery at Aberfeldy.

The 'Great Britain II' and 'Great Britain III' tours ran to a similar itinerary to 2007. In perfect weather conditions, LNER K4 2-6-0 No. 61994 *The Great Marquess* skirts Loch Carron, near Attadale with 'GBIII' on 12 April 2010.

BR Britannia Pacific No. 70013 *Oliver Cromwell* climbs away from the Tay Bridge past Wormit with the 'Great Britain II' on 13 April 2010.

The 'Great Britain IV' tour ran to Wick in 2011, but diesel hauled outwards from Inverness. LMS 'Black Five' 4-6-0s No. 45407 and No. 44871 return south over the Oykel viaduct at Invershin on 18 April.

A real stranger to the area, LMS Royal Scot 4-6-0 No. 46115 *Scots Guardsman* is seen at Inverness on 20 April 2011, having arrived from Edinburgh via Aberdeen.

Heading south from Inverness with a three coach empty stock movement, No. 46115 *Scots Guardsman* and LNER K4 2-6-0 No. 61994 *The Great Marquess* climb away from Culloden viaduct on 20 April 2011.

LNER K4 2-6-0 No. 61994 *The Great Marquess* crosses the second viaduct on the Horseshoe Curve, climbing towards County March summit with the Railway Touring Company's 'West Highlander' railtour returning from Fort William to Glasgow on 2 September 2007.

The Great Marquess has diesel assistance with Steam Dreams' 'Cathedrals Explorer' departing from Rannoch and crossing the viaduct on 20 May 2011.

Welcome to Rannoch sign.

LNER K4 2-6-0 No. 61994 *The Great Marquess* heads a Fort William – Mallaig photo charter away from Morar in October 2011.

LNER K4 2-6-0 No. 61994 *The Great Marquess* copes well with the 1-in-50 climb from Garve on the line to Kyle of Lochalsh on 20 May.

No. 61994 *The Great Marquess* crosses Clachnaharry swing bridge over the Caledonian Canal as it heads away from Inverness with Steam Dreams' 'Cathedrals Explorer' on 20 May 2012.

With the Isle of Skye in the background, No. 61994 *The Great Marquess* rounds the curve at Erbusaig on the approach to Kyle of Lochalsh.

LMS 'Black Five' 4-6-0 No. 45305 arrives at Garve with 'Great Britain V' on 23 April 2012 after stalling on the climb to Ravens' Rock.

No. 45305 departs from Garve on the 1-in-50 climb which starts at the platform end.

No. 45305 approaches the water stop at Achnasheen with 'Great Britain V'.

LMS 'Black Five' 4-6-0 No. 45305 crosses the end of Loch a'Chuilinn on the approach to Achanalt.

The end of the line; No. 45305 on arrival at Kyle of Lochalsh. From here, the passengers crossed to the Isle of Skye, then by ferry to Mallaig, continuing to Fort William on the other half of the train which had split into two portions at Thornton Junction the previous day.

LMS 'Black Five' 4-6-0 No. 45305 passes Loch Gowan on the climb from Achnasheen to the 646ft Luib summit.

LMS Royal Scot 4-6-0 No. 46115 *Scots Guardsman* crosses Findhorn viaduct over the River Findhorn through Strathdearn on the climb to Slochd, running from Inverness to Glasgow on 24 April 2012.

The first Royal Scot to work a passenger train on the Highland main line, No. 46115 arrives at Aviemore for a water stop.

Scots Guardsman storms through Dalwhinnie station on the climb to Drumochter.

LMS Royal Scot 4-6-0 No. 46115 *Scots Guardsman* accelerates downhill out of Pitlochry towards Perth with 'Great Britain V'. The two halves of the train would be reunited in Glasgow for a trip to Stranraer next day, before heading for Penzance and finally terminating at Paddington.

Steam Dreams' 2012 'Cathedrals Explorer' featured the unprecedented sight of LNER A1 Pacific No. 60163 *Tornado* on the Highland main line to Inverness. The A1 makes good progress up the mainly 1-in-70 climb to Drumochter summit on 19 May.

No. 60163 Tornado is on the Inverness – Aberdeen line, climbing from the crossing of the River Spey at Boat o'Brig towards Mulben on 22 May.

No. 60163 *Tornado* heads towards Dalnaspidal on the climb towards Drumochter, breasting the summit at 49.5mph with 11 coaches.